# ELTON JOHN / LEON RUSSELL

**WISE PUBLICATIONS**
part of The Music Sales Group
London / New York / Paris / Sydney / Copenhagen /
Berlin / Madrid / Hong Kong / Tokyo

Published by
**WISE PUBLICATIONS**
14-15 Berners Street, London W1T 3LJ, UK.

Exclusive distributors:
**MUSIC SALES LIMITED**
Distribution Centre, Newmarket Road, Bury St Edmunds, Suffolk, IP33 3YB, UK.
**MUSIC SALES PTY LIMITED**
20 Resolution Drive, Caringbah, NSW 2229, Australia.

Order No. AM1002342
ISBN 978-1-84938-866-5

This book © Copyright 2010 Wise Publications,
a division of Music Sales Limited.

Unauthorised reproduction of any part of this publication by
any means including photocopying is an infringement of copyright.

Arranged by Chris Hussey.
Edited by Jenni Wheeler.

Printed in the EU.

www.musicsales.com

IF IT WASN'T FOR BAD 10
EIGHT HUNDRED DOLLAR SHOES 5
HEY AHAB 18
GONE TO SHILOH 27
JIMMIE RODGERS' DREAM 34
THERE'S NO TOMORROW 41
MONKEY SUIT 46
THE BEST PART OF THE DAY 53
A DREAM COME TRUE 60
WHEN LOVE IS DYING 67
I SHOULD HAVE SENT ROSES 74
HEARTS HAVE TURNED TO STONE 82
NEVER TOO OLD (TO HOLD SOMEBODY) 89
IN THE HANDS OF ANGELS 96

**YOUR GUARANTEE OF QUALITY**

As publishers, we strive to produce every book to the highest
commercial standards. The music has been freshly engraved and
the book has been carefully designed to minimise awkward page
turns and to make playing from it a real pleasure.

Particular care has been given to specifying acid-free, neutral-sized
paper made from pulps which have not been elemental chlorine bleached.

This pulp is from farmed sustainable forests and was
produced with special regard for the environment.

Throughout, the printing and binding have been planned to ensure a sturdy,
attractive publication which should give years of enjoyment.

If your copy fails to meet our high standards, please inform us
and we will gladly replace it.

www.musicsales.com

# EIGHT HUNDRED DOLLAR SHOES

Words & Music by Elton John & Bernie Taupin

**With a relaxed lilt**

1. You had your grand il-lu-sion and wres-tled with your fate,

© Copyright 2010 Rouge Booze Incorporated, USA/HST Management Limited.
Universal Music Publishing Limited.
All rights in Germany administered by Universal Music Publ. GmbH.
All Rights Reserved. International Copyright Secured.

the winter of your dis-con-tent___ came twen-ty years too late.___

If it was love and I was there, I've for-got-ten where it

lives; we both stepped off a fro-zen rock on-to a burn-in' bridge.___ 2. You

came like an in-va-sion, all bells and whis-tles blow-in',___
(3.) bell-boys are cry-in', and mon-ey's chang-in' hands, your

reap - in' the re - wards\_\_ of the fa - ble you'd been sow - in'. I
cloak and dag - ger leg - a - cy's gone home to no man's land.\_\_ The

saw you cross\_\_ the land - ing,\_\_ de - scend - ing\_\_ mar - ble stairs, like
mar - quee lights are flick - er - ing, your pos - ter's fad - in' fast, like your

Cae - sar crossed the Ru - bi - con, you seemed to walk on air.\_\_
be - ing here just melts a - way like ice cubes in a glass.\_\_ And

yeah, I've seen your mo - vie, and I read it in your book.\_\_

*The truth just flew off ev-'ry page,* your songs have all the hooks. You're sev-en won-ders rolled in one, you shift-ed gear to cruise. Oh, you came to town in head-lines, and eight hun-dred dol-lar shoes.

Ooh, ooh. 3. Oh, the Oh, you came to town in head-lines, and eight hun-dred dol-lar shoes. Ooh, ooh, ooh.

# IF IT WASN'T FOR BAD

Words & Music by Leon Russell

right.___ Looked like an in-no-cent strang-er,___ but
some-thin' was just out of sight.___

How could I know___ that you would use me, fill out some plan___ of your
(4.) knew from the first___ night I met you, some-thin' just was-n't quite

Sheet music excerpt with lyrics:

own. I could-n't know you'd a-buse me, an'
right. Look like an in-no-cent strang-er,

leave me here hurt and a-lone.
some-thin' was just out of sight.

If it was-n't for you, I'd be hap-py. If it

wasn't for lies,\_\_ you'd be true. I know that you could be\_\_ just like you should; if it wasn't for bad,\_\_ you'd be good.\_\_

*To Coda* ⊕

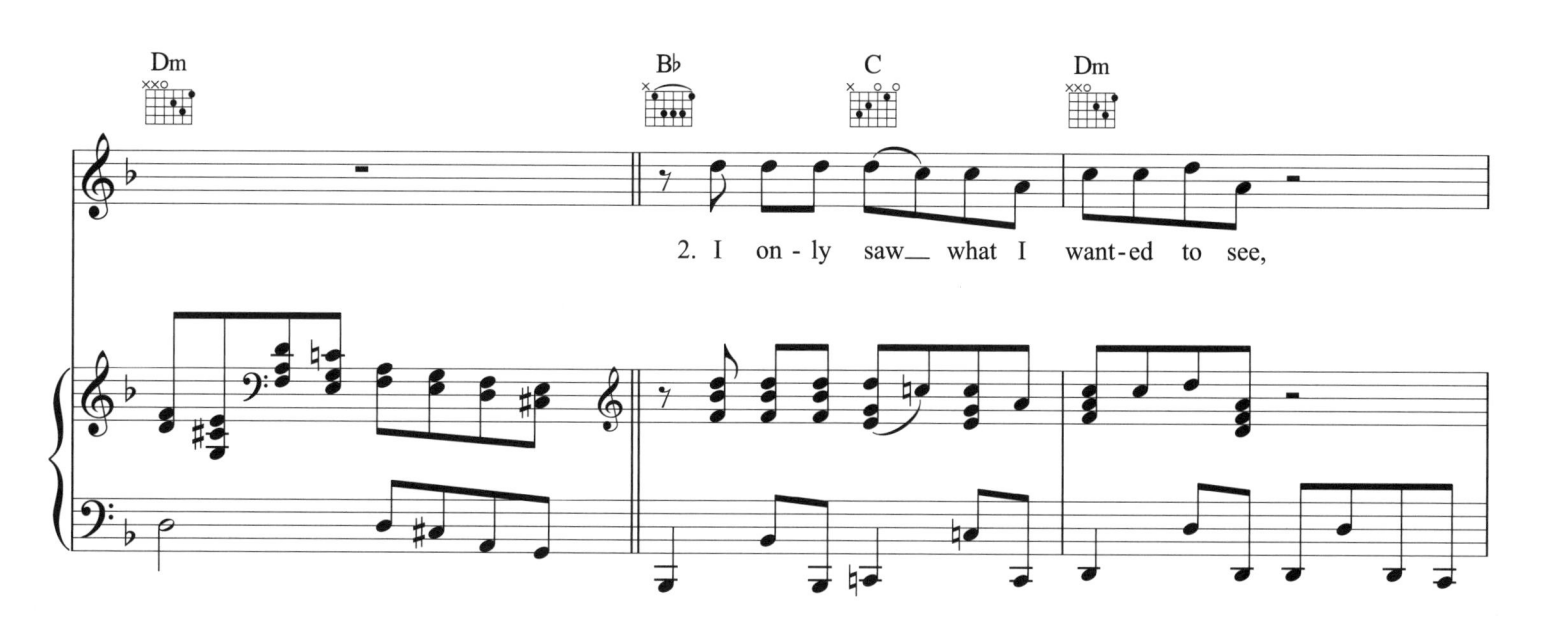

2. I only saw\_\_ what I wanted to see,

you were a dream in my mind. I didn't know how you real-ly could be, it did-n't take long for me to find.

3. I guess that it's my fault for see-in' on-ly what I want-ed to see.

I could-n't know you would be a play-er just act-in' for me.

If it was-n't for you, I'd be hap-py. If it was-n't for lies, you'd be true.

I know you could be just like you should; if it

was-n't for bad,— you'd be good.—

*Ah,—* *ah,—*

*ah.—*

*Ah,—*

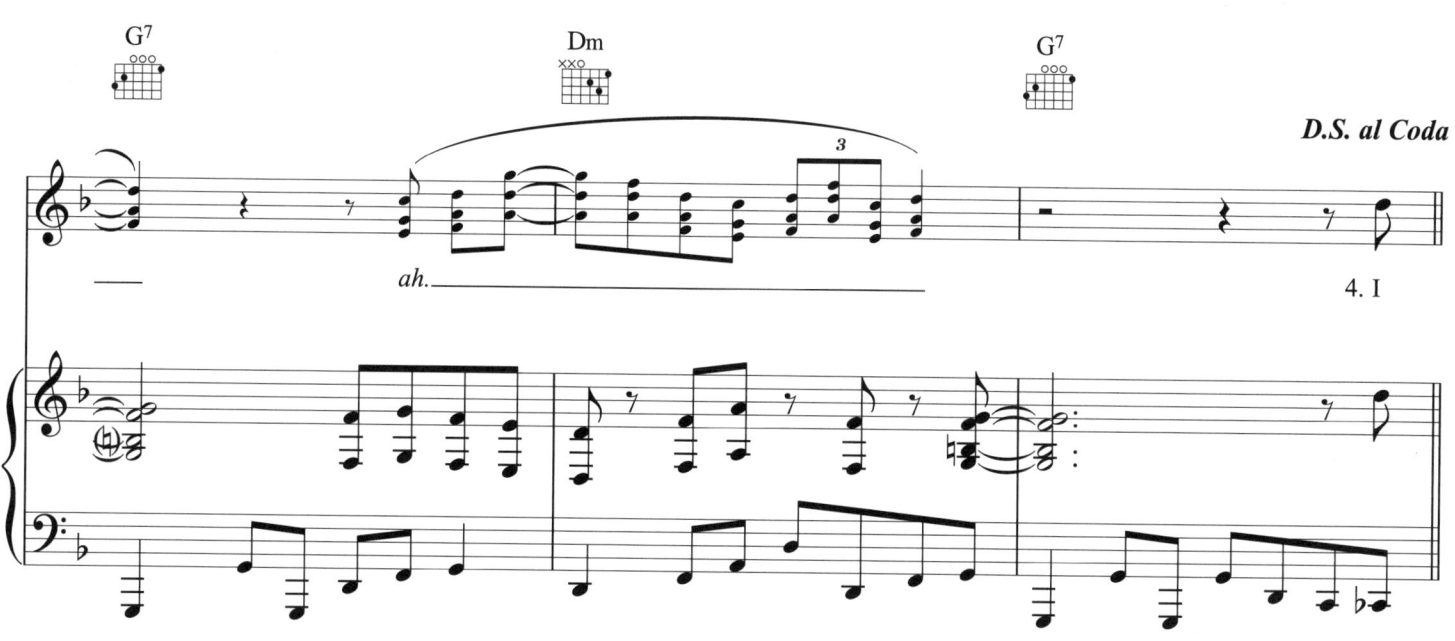

*ah.___* 

*Ah,___*

*ah.___*

4. I

**D.S. al Coda**

⊕ *Coda*

If it was-n't for bad,___ you'd be good.___

# HEY AHAB

Words & Music by Elton John & Bernie Taupin

© Copyright 2010 Rouge Booze Incorporated, USA/HST Management Limited.
Universal Music Publishing Limited.
All rights in Germany administered by Universal Music Publ. GmbH.
All Rights Reserved. International Copyright Secured.

1. It's a constant struggle gettin' up that hill, there's a change of guard ev'ry day.
2. In a crumblin' city, we were trapped for days, with a broken sun above the

Lyrics:

When you're clingin' on to a driftwood boat, you pray a great white whale might come your way. No freeway traffic in the frozen North, just a chain-link fence full of birds. And when the

Caught like Jonah, forty fathoms down, and a sign on the wall said, 'hope allowed'. All the cryptic symbols carved on a bone, mm, a far cry from a tattooed rose. And when the

har - poon's load - ed in the can - on bay, you'll be roll -
boys in the rig - gin' in catch the wind, we'll all weigh

- in' through the pa - ges lost for words.
an - chor and it's West - ward a - Ho!___

Hey,___ hey,___ A - hab, can you tell___

___ me where I can catch a ride___ out___ of here? Hey,-

_A - hab, mm, hoist that sail, you got-ta stand up straight when you ride that whale._

23

(Lyrics)

Hey, hey, hey, — A-hab, can you tell — me where I can catch a ride — out — of here? Oo-oo, hey, — A-hab, mm, — hoist that sail, you gotta stand up straight when you ride that whale. — Hey, — A-hab, can you tell —

*— me where I can catch a ride out of here? Hey, — A-hab, mm, — hoist that sail, you gotta stand up straight when you ride — that, mm, — whale.* Vocal ad lib.

Cm7
3fr
F/C
Repeat ad lib.
Cm
3fr
F/C
Hey, A - hab, hey, A - hab, A - - - - hab!
1-3.
Cm
3fr
Cm7
3fr
Hey, A - hab, hey, A - hab, hey,
F/C
A - hab.
Repeat ad lib.
4.
Cm
3fr
ad lib.

# GONE TO SHILOH

Words & Music by Elton John & Bernie Taupin

Funereally ♩ = 66

© Copyright 2010 Rouge Booze Incorporated, USA/HST Management Limited.
Universal Music Publishing Limited.
All rights in Germany administered by Universal Music Publ. GmbH.
All Rights Reserved. International Copyright Secured.

1. Lu - ther left us first light Friday morn - ing,
(3.) old black roos - ter sang him down that dirt road. His

lit - tle Dan and Beck - y waved good - bye. They're gon - na
step seemed bold, his man - ner fan - cy - free. I pray we

have to share the weight to-geth-er; i-dle hands will see a good farm slow-ly
see him 'live and well in the fall here, than that God for-sa-ken place in Ten-nes-

die.
-see.

Gone to Shi-loh for the u-nion, shoul-der to shoul-der, side

__ by side.__ Gone to Shi - loh;__ hope springs e - ter - nal__ when
*2° men stand u - nit - ed__*}

flags and bul-lets start to fly.__

2. A - pril's come__ and the air smells__ fresh with rain, they watched his shad-ow fade a-round the bend.__

He's head-ed for a diff-'rent kind of thun-der, and the stunned sur-prise in the eyes of dy-ing men.

Gone to Shi-loh for the u-nion, shoul-der to shoul-der, side by side.

Gone to Shi - loh; time pass - es slow - ly when flags and bul - lets start to fly.

*D.S. al Coda*

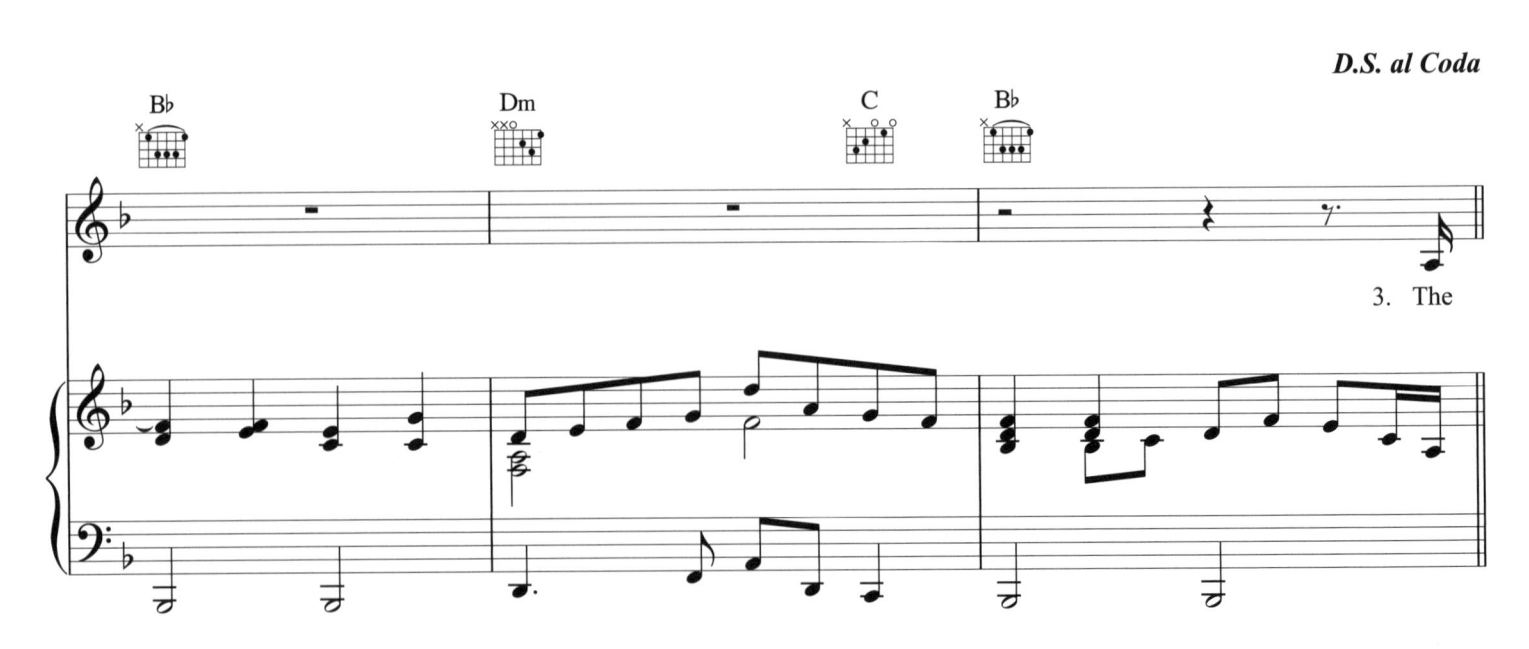

3. The

*Coda*

After all of this, if we should prevail, heaven help the South when Sherman comes their way.

# JIMMIE RODGERS' DREAM

Words & Music by Elton John, T-Bone Burnett & Bernie Taupin

Country ♩ = 84

1. I'm lookin' at a fu-n'ral wag-on rollin' down

© Copyright 2010 Rouge Booze Incorporated, USA/HST Management Limited.
Universal Music Publishing Limited (75%) (All rights in Germany administered by Universal Music Publ. GmbH)/Copyright Control (25%).
All Rights Reserved. International Copyright Secured.

two-lane highway ever-windin' past a desert town. A big blue canvas painted by the Master's hand, the shiftin' clouds above and endless miles of sand.

2. In that mir-ror, may-be that's what's left of me,— wheez-ing
(3.) dust-y beat-en Del-ta boys cut-tin' heads,— a

like a freight train haul-ing six-ty tons of steel. In
black face carn-y show-man scare a song to death.

Air 'em out's the best re-lease and get some rest. Car-rie,
my short life, I've seen as much as most men need. Now,

don't wait up for me, the brake-man's go-in' west.
I'm just look-in' for some clean-er air to breathe.

In this room, all a-lone, I dream of you.

In this drawer, I found some-one I nev-er knew. Now, I

pop a top,— and stay up late— with Gid-e-on,—

fall a-sleep to visions of— mer-id - i - an.—

3. I've seen

**2.**

Far a-way,— far a-way, so many years,— so many days... All a-long— this bro-ken land,— I've seen a lov-er's emp-ty arms, and hung-er's emp-ty hands.

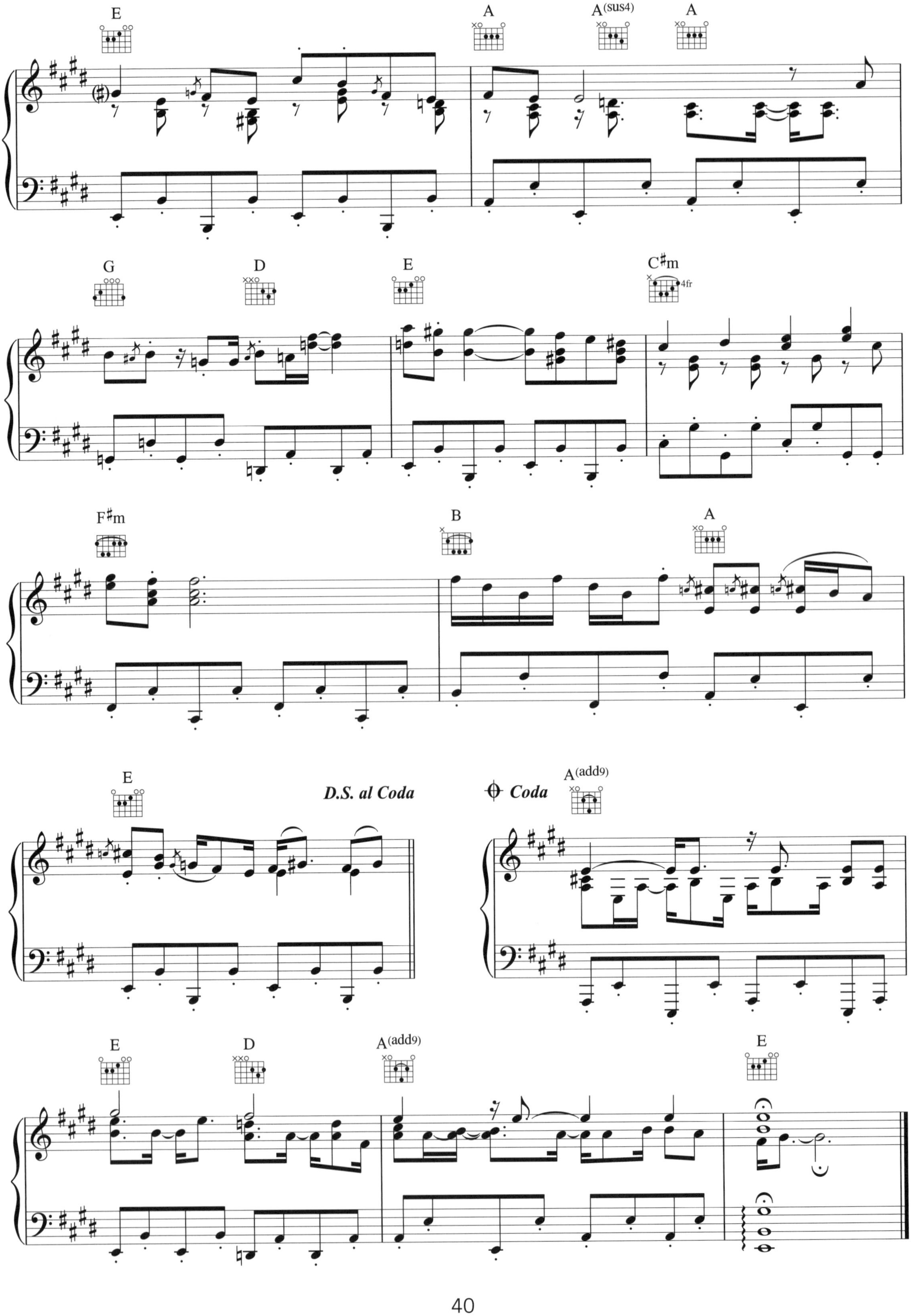
E
A
A(sus4)
A
G
D
E
C♯m
4fr
F♯m
B
A
E
D.S. al Coda
Coda
A(add9)
E
D
A(add9)
E

# THERE'S NO TOMORROW

Words & Music by Elton John, Leon Russell, T-Bone Burnett
& James Shaw

Sombre waltz ♩= 90

1. There's no time for waitin', no future to see. Inside
(2.) all know the story, we've heard it before. We

© Copyright 2010 HST Management Limited.
Universal Music Publishing Limited (16.68%) (All rights in Germany administered by Universal Music Publ. GmbH)/Copyright Control (83.32%).
All Rights Reserved. International Copyright Secured.

A♭
B♭m
A♭
E♭
— the next mo - ment, noth- in' might be. The
end up, no ques - tion, out - side of death's door. There's
C7
B♭m
Fm
an - swer's not cer - tain, no time to de - cide is
no eas - y an - swer to the ques - tion at hand; so
A♭
B♭m
C
Dm7(♭5)
C/E
this the last cur - tain; there's no place to hide.
eas - y to ask and not un - der - stand.

Fm

There's no to-mor - row,

C7

there's no to-mor - row, there's

Fm

no to-mor - row, there's

on - ly to - day.___ 2. We

B♭m/F
B♭m
C7(sus4)
D.S. al Coda
Coda
C
Ddim
C/E
Fm
Oh.
There's
3
molto rit.
C7
Fm
B♭m
Fm
on - - ly to - day.

# MONKEY SUIT

Words & Music by Elton John & Bernie Taupin

**Driving Rock** ♩ = 116

1. If you're look-in' for the glor-
(2.) -der to the moon,

© Copyright 2010 Rouge Booze Incorporated, USA/HST Management Limited.
Universal Music Publishing Limited.
All rights in Germany administered by Universal Music Publ. GmbH.
All Rights Reserved. International Copyright Secured.

*-y,           you think\_\_ that  you\_\_ might find,\_\_\_        in a bul-
\_\_\_        beat on\_\_ that sa - cred drum,\_\_\_          tram-ple on\_\_

- let - rid - dled stol - en  car   on a back road in The Pines.\_\_\_
\_\_ the hands of those that cling  to  ev - 'ry rung.\_\_\_

If it's round,\_\_ just like\_\_ a  med - al      on a tired\_\_
Ev-'ry seed\_\_ you crush\_\_ be - neath,\_\_\_          like stone\_\_

*old man of war,* ____ or hid-den like that Bur-ma Star
*ground in a mill.* ____ You nev-er drew a de-cent breath,

in my dad's bot-tom drawer.
but you're just dressed to kill.

Look at you in your mon-key suit, driv-in' south, noth-in' left to prove. You come back here in your cow-boy boots, oh, dressed to kill in your mon-key suit. Ev-'ry pose you strike, ev-'ry

frame they shoot, shows you dressed to kill___ in your mon-key suit.

2. Build your lad -

Shoo shoo shoo shoo, I did-n't ring.

A7
Shoo shoo shoo shoo, I did-n't ring. Shoo shoo shoo
1.
D7
shoo, I did-n't ring. Shoo shoo shoo shoo, I did-n't ring.
2.
D7
D.S. al Coda
Coda
D7
Shoo shoo shoo shoo, I did-n't ring.

G7
Shoo shoo shoo shoo, I did-n't ring. Shoo shoo shoo
shoo, I did-n't ring.
D7
Shoo shoo shoo shoo, I did-n't ring.
1.
Shoo shoo shoo shoo, I did-n't ring.
2.
D7
shoo, I did-n't ring. Ev-

-'ry pose you strike, ev-'ry frame they shoot, shows you dressed to kill

in your mon-key suit, mon-key suit,

mon-key suit,

mon-key suit.

# THE BEST PART OF THE DAY

Words & Music by Elton John & Bernie Taupin

**Steadily** ♩ = 69

1. I hear you singin', "I shall be released," like a chain-saw runnin' through a
2. There's a canyon where an echo hangs, like the ancient bells of

© Copyright 2010 Rouge Booze Incorporated, USA/HST Management Limited.
Universal Music Publishing Limited.
All rights in Germany administered by Universal Music Publ. GmbH.
All Rights Reserved. International Copyright Secured.

masterpiece. But that's alright, that's o.k., grab the
Notre Dame. It's beyond the hills, out of sight, thought I

bottle and slide my way. You dreamt of a devil
heard 'em ringin' all last night. Hear the mating call of the

down below, sprinkled cayenne pepper in your
morning dove, like Romeo angels in the

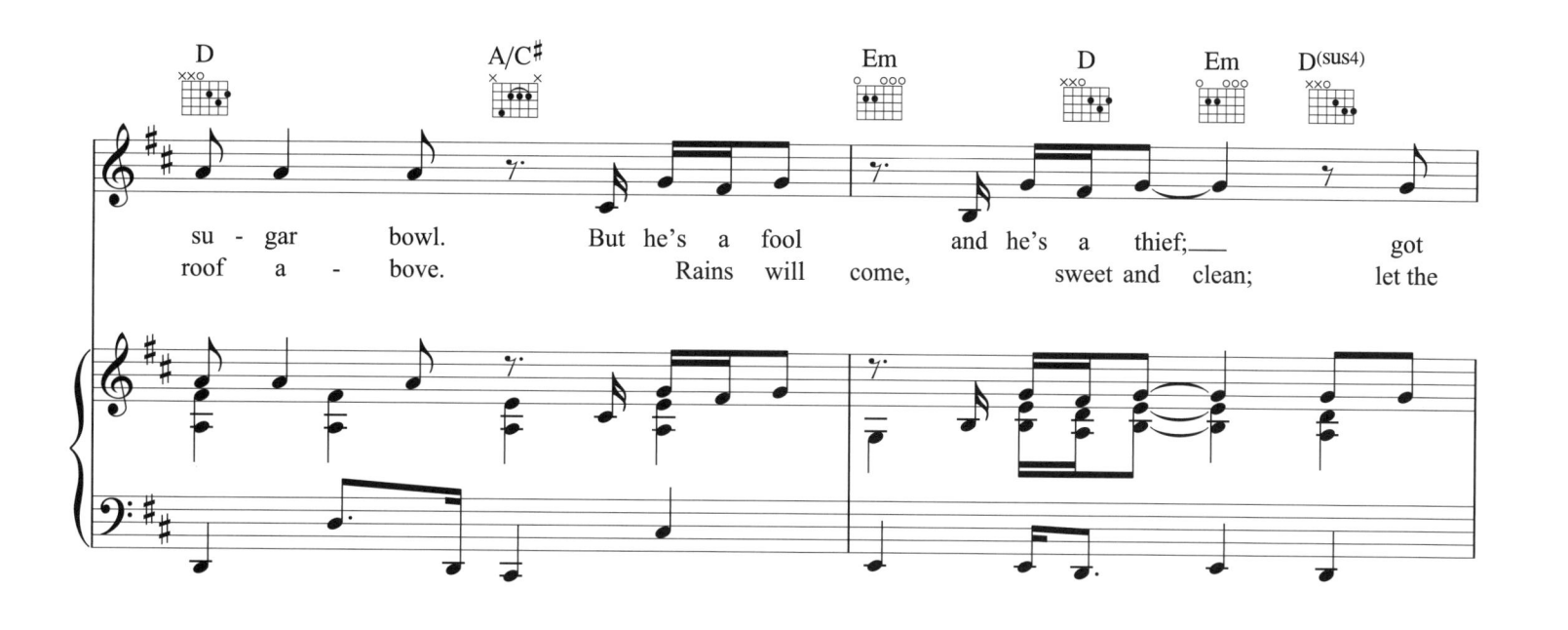

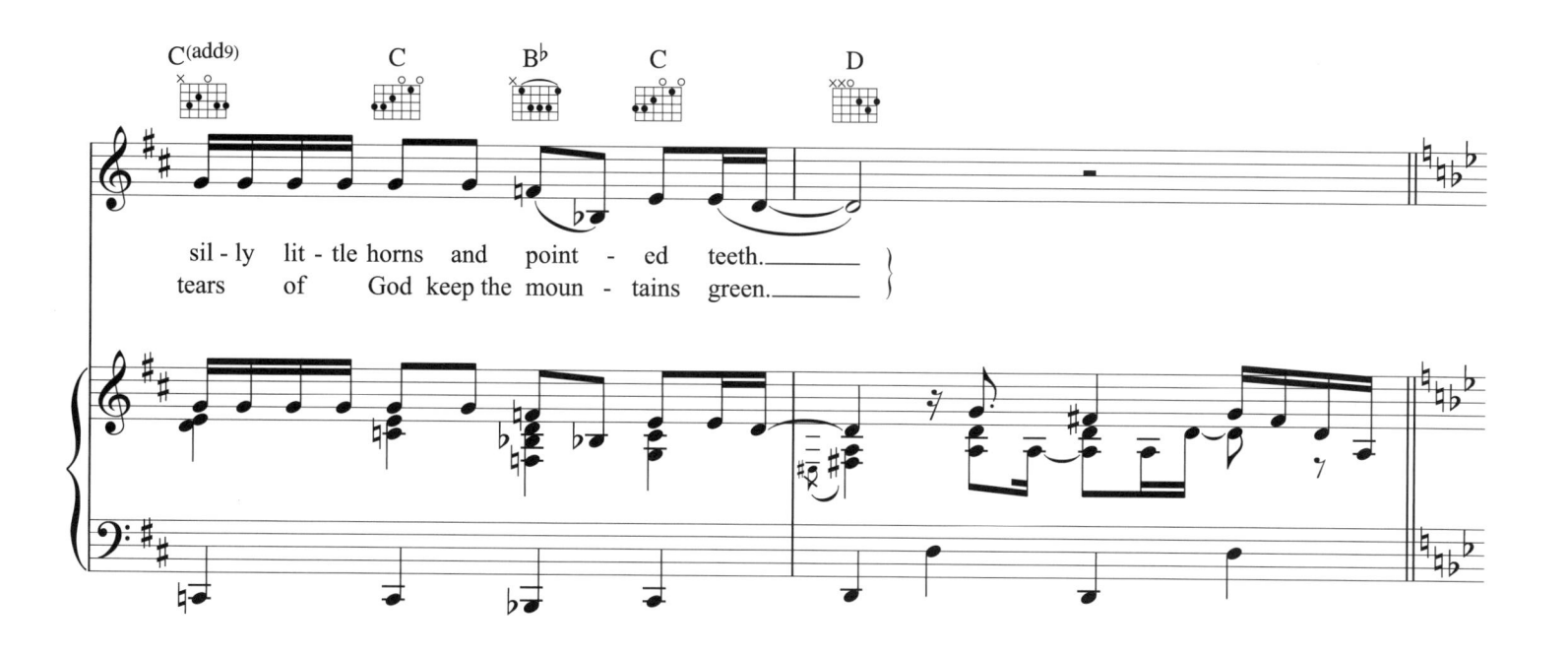

| D | A/C# | Em D | Em D(sus4) |

su - gar bowl. But he's a fool and he's a thief;___ got
roof a - bove. Rains will come, sweet and clean; let the

| C(add9) | C | B♭ C | D |

sil - ly lit - tle horns and point - ed teeth._____
tears of God keep the moun - tains green._____

| E♭ | A♭/E♭ E♭ | B♭ |

Roll back the cov - ers and raise the shades,___

| Cm | D(sus4) | D | Gm | B♭/F |

we don't want to miss out on the best part of the day. You're my

| E♭ | B♭/D | Cm7 | E♭/B♭ |

best friend, you shared my cra-zy ways; now we

| A♭ | E♭/G | A♭ | F/A | B♭ | E♭/B♭ | B♭ |

don't want to miss out on the best part of the day.

| D | F#m | G |

One big sun com-in' up, old moon go-in' down,___ thun-der break-in' in the east, I'm gon-na love you 'til it comes a-round.___

E♭ A♭/E♭ E♭ B♭
Roll back the cov - ers and raise the shades,
Cm D(sus4) D Gm B♭/F
we don't want to miss out on the best part of the day. You're my
E♭ B♭/D Cm7 E♭/B♭
best friend, you shared my cra - zy ways; now we
A♭ E♭/G A♭ F/A
don't want to miss out on the best part of the day.
6fr
4fr
3fr

You're my best friend, you shared my cra-zy ways; now we don't want to miss out on the best part of the day.

# A DREAM COME TRUE

Words & Music by Elton John & Leon Russell

**Upbeat blues** ♩ = 116

1. I can hear your heart pounding in my ear. Now, I feel the sound and the time is near. I feel the
(2.) so complete with the things you do. And the music's sweet, you make me feel brand new. I hear the

© Copyright 2010 HST Management Limited.
Universal Music Publishing Limited (50%) (All rights in Germany administered by Universal Music Publ. GmbH)/Copyright Control (50%).
All Rights Reserved. International Copyright Secured.

taste of all the things you do.
sound, songs start com-ing through.

Now the time has come; I know you're a dream come true.
Some-how I know that you're a dream come true.

2. You make me

And it

takes my breath, when it sounds that way. Seems like you chase the clouds a-way. And I feel so good each and ev-'ry day. Life is good, each and ev-'ry way. 3. Now I feel the beat of the danc-ing drums. 'N' now I know we're gon-na have some fun. Now the time stands still___ and the blues are through.___

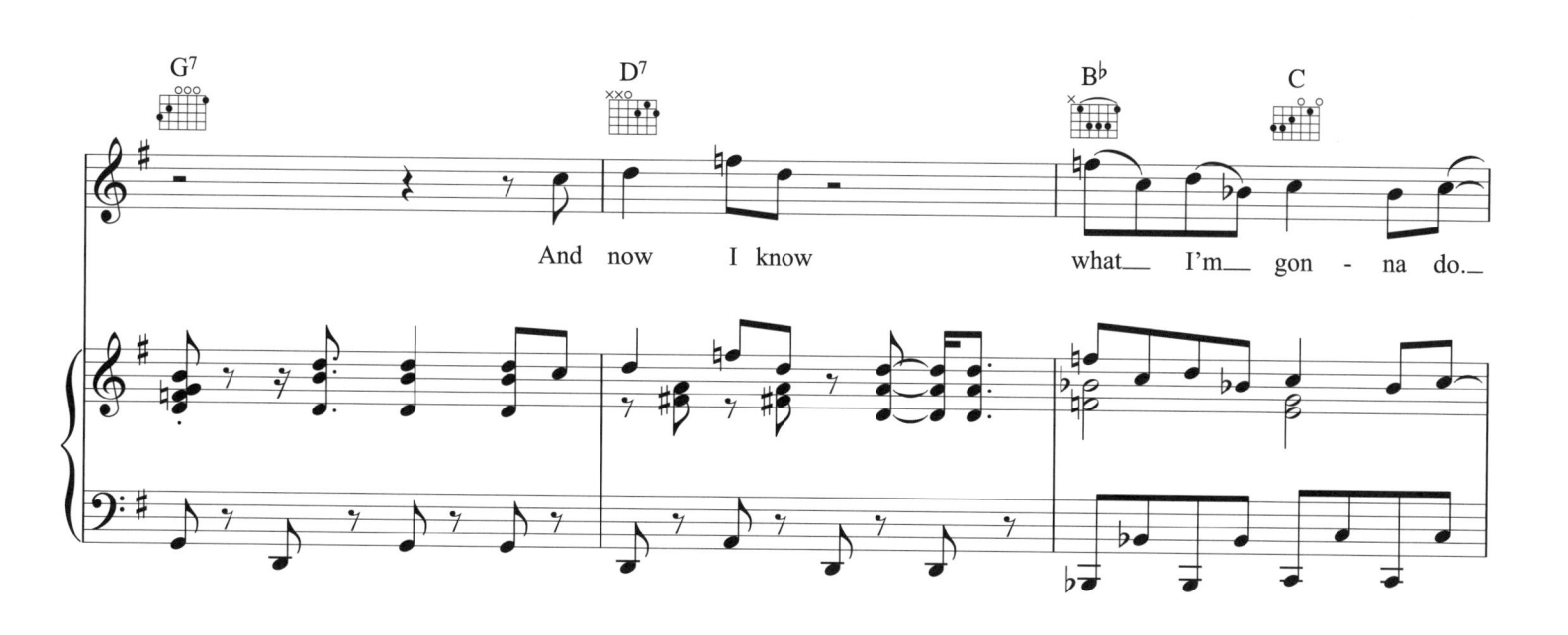

And now I know what___ I'm___ gon-na do.___

Oh___ yeah.___ *Ah,___*

*ah,* *ah,* *ah,* *ah,* *ah,* *ah.*

Now I Oh, it takes my breath, when it sounds that way. And it seems like you can chase the clouds a-way. And I feel so good in each and ev - 'ry way,___ and life is good,___ each and

ev - 'ry day.___

D7
B♭
C
G7
G7 C/D G7 C/D G7 C/D G7 C/D
Ooh, ooh, ooh.
sim.
G7 C/D G7 C/D G7 C/D G7 C/D G7 C/D G7 C/D
Ooh, ooh, ooh.
Ooh, ooh, ooh.
Play 6 x then ad lib.
disintegration
G7 C/D G7 C/D G7 C/D G7 C/D G7 C/D G7 C/D
Ooh, ooh, ooh.

# WHEN LOVE IS DYING

Words & Music by Elton John & Bernie Taupin

**Pensively and steadily** ♩ = 63

1. They say we bruise too eas-i-ly; I don't know if that's the way for me. I've seen 'em come, I've seen 'em go, I've

© Copyright 2010 Rouge Booze Incorporated, USA/HST Management Limited.
Universal Music Publishing Limited.
All rights in Germany administered by Universal Music Publ. GmbH.
All Rights Reserved. International Copyright Secured.

seen ev-'ry-one I know fall in and out of love; it's just the way it goes.

Word is out, si-lence seems so loud;
(2.) pain you nev-er can ex-plain, it

there's no light a-bove or be-low me now. I've seen it grow, I've seen it live,
cuts so deep, time and time a-gain. I felt it then, I feel it now, but

I've seen ev-'ry-thing I give fall-in' out my hands; no mat-ter who I'm
no-bod-y told me how to fight a world of hurt; some-bod-y help

F7
E♭
with.
me now.
And no - bod - y ev - er tells you when love is dy -
F
F(sus4)
F
B♭
- ing. When love is dy - ing, it just
B♭7
E♭
Gm/D
Cm7
gets a lit - tle cold - er. And we stop try - ing, we stop try - ing, yeah, we stop
B♭
F/A
Gm
Gm/F
E♭
try - ing. Oh,

when love is dy - ing.

2. There's a

dy - ing. But

love nev-er gets to show you, and I nev-er got to know you. No, we never stood a chance when love was dy-ing. No, love nev-er makes it eas-y, 'n' I nev-er got that feel-in'; no, we never stood a chance when love was dying. 'N' nobody ever tells you when love is dying. When love is dying, it just gets a little colder. And we stop trying, we stop trying, yeah, we stop trying.

Gm
Gm/F
E♭
6fr
F
Oh,
when love is
B♭
B♭/A
Gm
Gm/F
E♭
6fr
F
dy-ing,
oh,
when love is
E♭
6fr
molto rit.
B♭
dy-ing.

# I SHOULD HAVE SENT ROSES

Words & Music by Leon Russell & Bernie Taupin

Steadily ♩ = 76

1. Are you stand-ing out-side,

lookin' up at the sky,___ cursin'___ a wanderin'___ star?___

Well, if I were you,___ I'd throw rocks at___ the moon.___ I'd say, "Damn you___ wherever___ you are". I don't know where to start.___

This cage 'round my heart locked up what I meant to say, what I felt all along the way. Just wonderin' how come I couldn't take your breath away? 'Cause I never sent ro-

-ses,\_\_\_ I nev-er did e-nough.\_\_\_

I did-n't know how to love_____ you,\_\_\_\_\_

though I loved you so much.\_\_\_\_

And I should have sent ro-ses\_\_\_

Dm7
E7
Am
when you crossed my mind,
Am/G
F
Dm7
for no oth - er rea - son
than the fact you were mine.
E(sus4)
To Coda
E7
Am
C/G
I should have sent ro - ses.
F
C/E
Am
C/G
Fmaj7
2. Look- in' back on my life,

oh, if fate should de-cide, I could do it all o-ver a-gain. I'd build no more walls, I'd stay true and re-call fra-grance of you on the winds. You'll get bet-ter than me,

Fmaj7
Dm7
E7
Am
some - one who can see.
C/G
Fmaj7
Right from the start give you all that you need.
C/E
Dm7
E7
I'll slip a-way,
know-in' I'm half the man
F
E(sus4)
E
D.S. al Coda
I should be.
'Cause I nev - er sent ro -

*Coda*

I should have sent ro - ses.

Yeah, I should have sent ro - ses.

# HEARTS HAVE TURNED TO STONE

Words & Music by Leon Russell

**Driving blues** ♩ = 96

Oh, yeah. 1. I'm out here in the darkness, I
(2.) Now the sun is rising

hear the howl-in' wind. Some-times I sit and won-der, will I
high-er in the sky, the morn-ing light is crawl-ing from the

© Copyright 2010 Copyright Control.
All Rights Reserved. International Copyright Secured.

82

A7
ev - er see love a - gain?
dark-ness of the night.
Look - in' for an an - swer, not an
The rain - drops keep on fall - ing, there
G
Em7
A
G
eas - y thing to find.
is no light of day.
Oh,
Em7
A
B7
yeah.
Out here in the wil - der - ness, with
The sad - ness deep in - side me

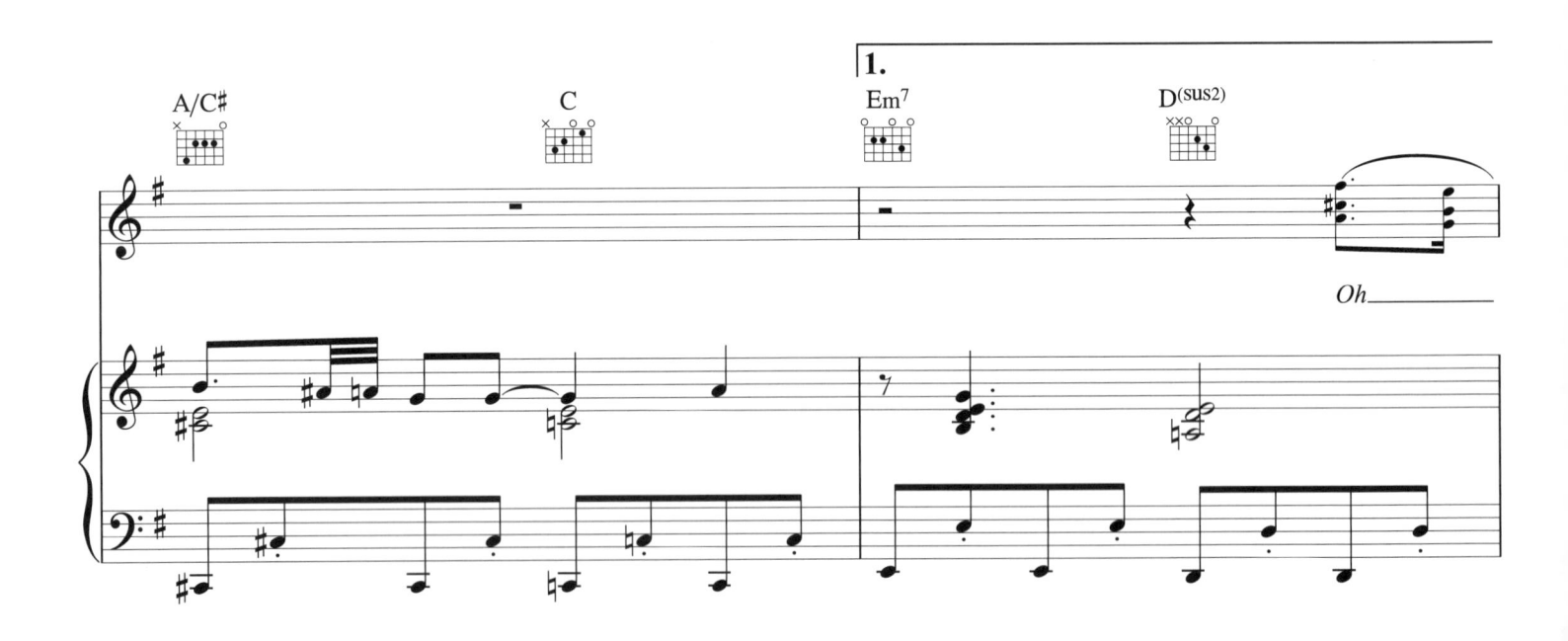

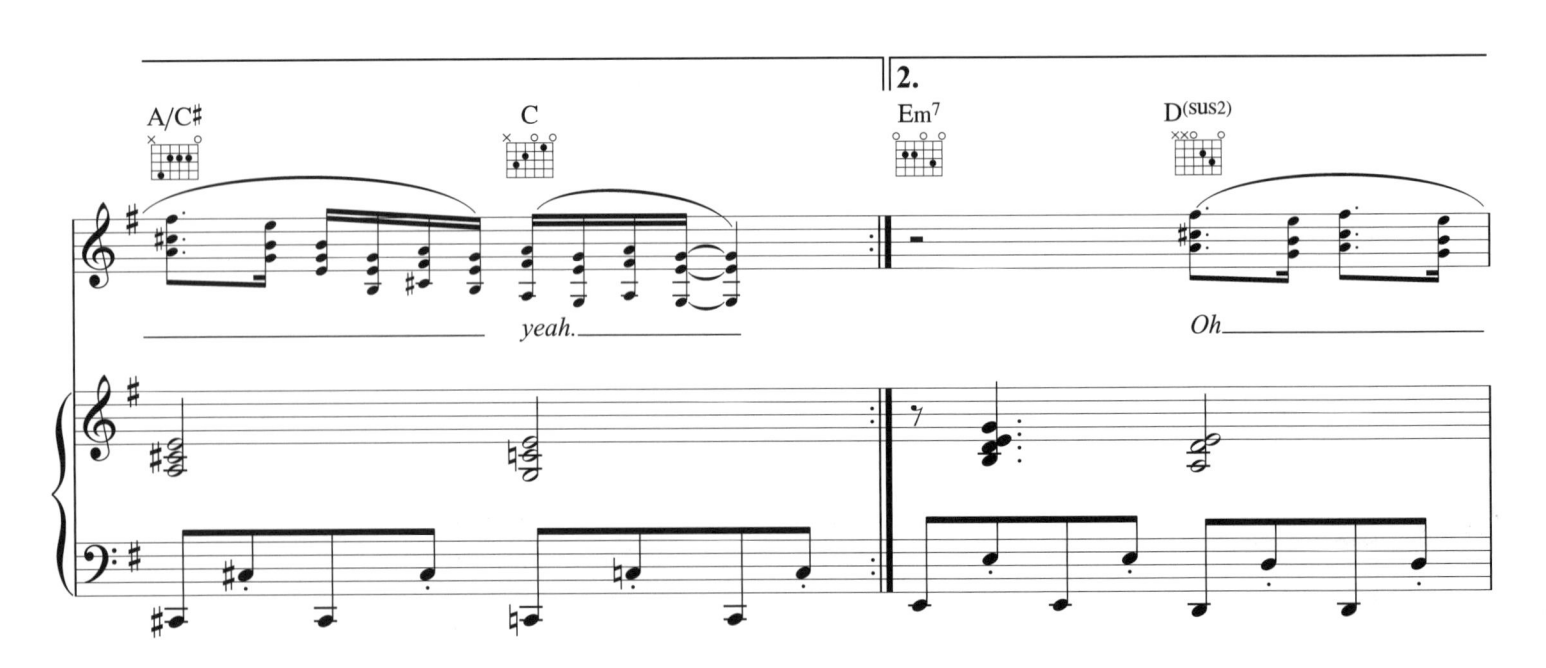

ques - tions on my mind.
does - n't seem to go a - way.

*Oh*

*yeah.*

*Oh*

A/C#
C
A
yeah.
And there's no way out,
2º piano solo 'til *
Em7
no road home; I'm lost in doubt and I'm
A
all a - lone. The time has come when
B
love is done, the hearts have fi - n'ly turned to stone.
3

* 3, 4. No more bright tomorrow, only sad today. My heart is filled with sorrow, the pain won't go away. {Just Try / try} to keep from cryin' all night long and through the day.

Lost and all alone, (the/and) hearts have fi-n'ly turned to stone. *Yeah.* *Oh, yeah.*

2.
Em A Em A Em A Em A
Yeah.
Em A Em A Em Em/D
Oh,
A/C♯ C
yeah.
1.
Em Em/D A/C♯ C
2.
Em
Yeah!

# NEVER TOO OLD
# (TO HOLD SOMEBODY)

Words & Music by Elton John & Bernie Taupin

**Tenderly** ♩ = 60

1. Don't a-ban-don the light, don't step a-way, don't give up that tune that you nev-er could play. If you're
2. Don't think you've gone out, don't flick-er and fade; if you're gon-na get lem-ons, then you do what they say.

© Copyright 2010 Rouge Booze Incorporated, USA/HST Management Limited.
Universal Music Publishing Limited.
All rights in Germany administered by Universal Music Publ. GmbH.
All Rights Reserved. International Copyright Secured.

[G] fold-ing your tent, / Wind makes you wear-y, [B7] and the gas-pipes groan, / oh, it knocks you a-round. if

[Em] ev-'ry bone rat-tles / Logs on the fire [Em/D] [C] through nights all a-lone. / beat sun shin-in' down. Well, you're / But you're

[Bm/D] tough-er than leath-er, / hard-er than nails, [Am7/D] no old bur-lap sack, / no skin-ny old tack, not some / you're still

hard scrab-ble weed  grow - in' up through the cracks.
sharp as a ra - zor, and I like you like that.

Don't you know, you're nev-er too old, nev-er too old to hold some-bod-y? Don't you know, you're nev-er too old, nev-er too old to hold some - bod-y? You're nev-er too old to hold some - bod-y.

I could bet on a horse, but I'm bet-tin' on

you.___ You've still got what it takes,___ you got noth-in', noth-in' to pro - o - - - - - ove. You're nev-er too old,___ nev-er too old___ to hold___ some-

-body. Don't you know, you're nev-er too old, nev-er too old to hold_____ some-bod-y? Oh, you're nev-er too old___ to hold_____ some-

C/G
G
F
C/E
-bod - y,
mm,
some -
rit. poco a poco
C/G
G
F
C/E
Cm/E♭
-bod - y,
mm,
Cm
3fr
C/G
G
mm,
some - -
bod - y.
3
3

# IN THE HANDS OF ANGELS

Words & Music by Leon Russell

I could have giv-en up, and not tried to make it to to-mor-row, like a bro-ken heart-ed lov-er.
when I woke on that first day. There was noth-in' I could say; I was in the hands of an-gels.

2. But there was a brand new start, sud-den-ly I was ta-ken new and far a-way plac-es,
4. John-ny and the Gov-'nor came and brought me to my sense. They made me feel just like a king,

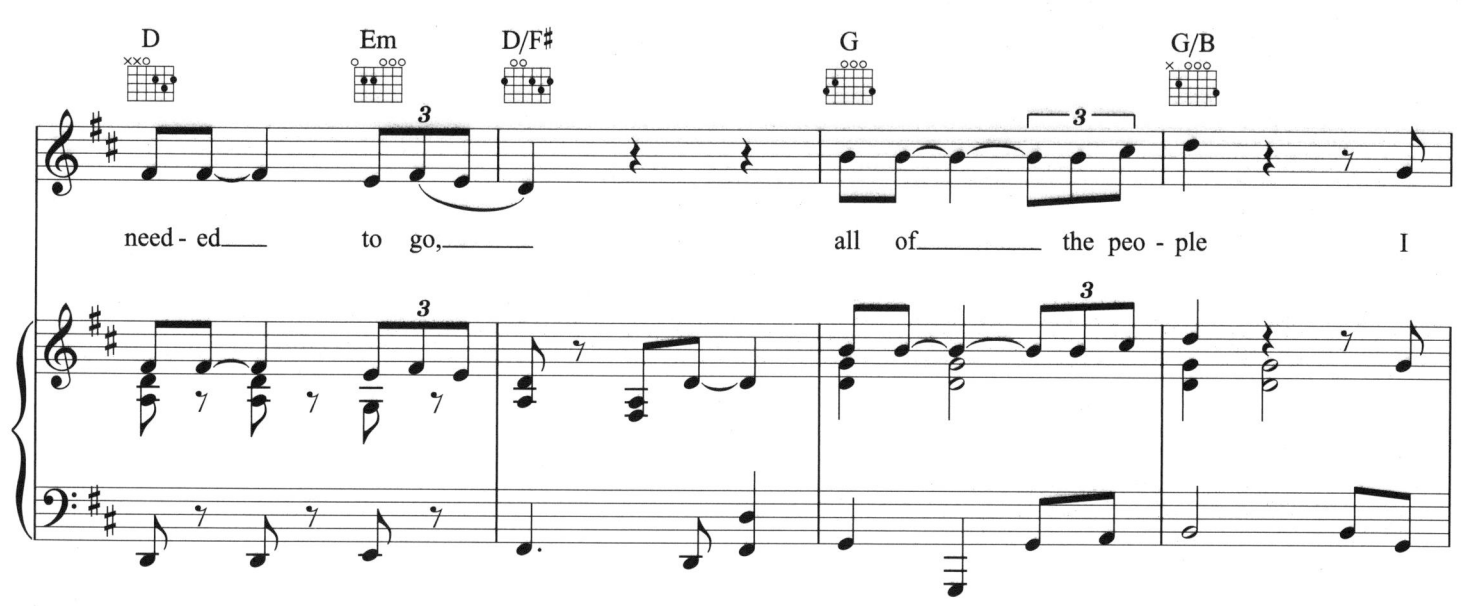

and the mu - sic I_____ was sha - ken._____
made me lose all my bad de - fence._____

3. It
5. And they knew all_____ the plac - es_____ I

need - ed_____ to go,_____ all of_____ the peo - ple I

D A7/E D/F# G A G/B A/C#
need - ed to know. They knew who I need - ed and
D Bm Em
who need - ed me, and who would come help me, and who would
D/A Aaug A D A7
just let me be. I was in the hands of an -
D Em D/F# G A
- gels un - til this ver - - y day.

D/F♯ D Em D/F♯ G A D/F♯
In - side the hands of an - gels,
Bm Em Asus4
what more can I say?
A D A7 D Em
When you're in the hands of an - gels,
D7/F♯ G A7 D/F♯
life is oh, so sweet.

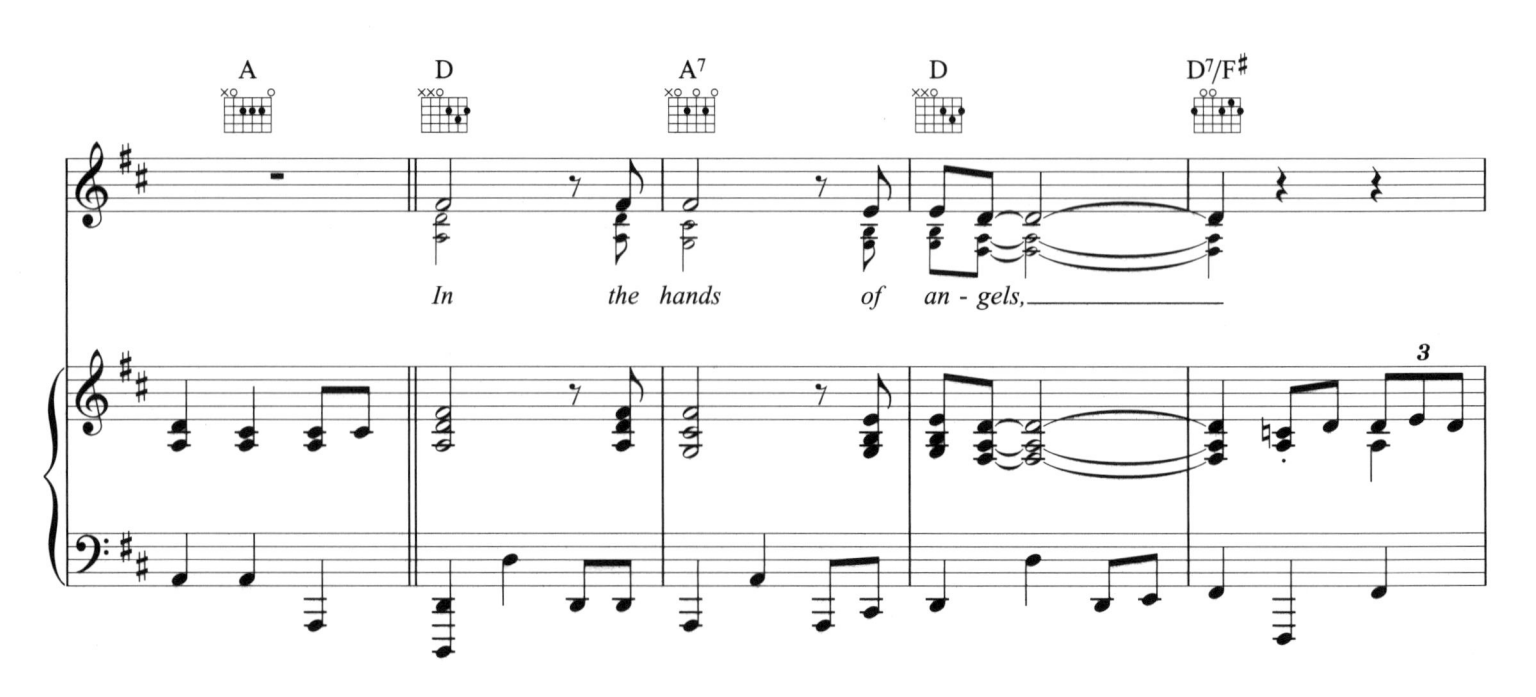

And you feel the love____ down deep in-side, e-ven out there on____ the street.____

*In the hands of an-gels,____*

G
A
D/F♯
D
Em7
D/F♯
G
A
ooh,
ooh,
ooh.
Ah,
ah,
straight ♪s
D/F♯
Bm
Em
D/A
A7
ah,
ah.
G
C9
D
Ooh,
ooh,
ooh.



1 2 3 4 5 6 7 8 9

# Bringing you the words and the music

All the latest music in print... rock & pop plus jazz, blues, country, classical and the best in West End show scores.

- Books to match your favourite CDs.

- Book-and-CD titles with high quality backing tracks for you to play along to. Now you can play guitar or piano with your favourite artist... or simply sing along!

- Audition songbooks with CD backing tracks for both male and female singers for all those with stars in their eyes.

- Can't read music? No problem, you can still play all the hits with our wide range of chord songbooks.

- Check out our range of instrumental tutorial titles, taking you from novice to expert in no time at all!

- Musical show scores include *The Phantom Of The Opera*, *Les Misérables*, *Mamma Mia* and many more hit productions.

- DVD master classes featuring the techniques of top artists.

Visit your local music shop or, in case of difficulty, contact the Marketing Department, Music Sales Limited, Newmarket Road, Bury St Edmunds, Suffolk, IP33 3YB, UK
marketing@musicsales.co.uk